ASHES TO LIGHT

Poems by
VICTOR ALARCÓN

Collected by
**JONITA
ALARCÓN**

"Slick" Vic Publishing

Ashes to Light
Poems by Victor Alarcón
Collected by Jonita Alarcón

Publisher:
"Slick" Vic Publishing

ISBN:

Cover Art:

Printed in the United States of
America

First Edition

For everyone who has ever paused over a line of poetry and felt a little less alone.

And to Victor—

Thank you for the words you left behind.

We hope these poems bring peace to all who read them.

Thank you to Albert and Darla Alarcon for all their help in making this book possible.

Table of Contents

Introduction

Victor started writing poems and song lyrics, at a very young age.

He wrote about his personal experiences, and his dreams.

Some were sad, and some had happy endings.

He loved life and lived it his own way.

This book is his dream come true.

Juice

People are juice.
I know myself.
Come see through the eyes
Of somebody else.

The whispers to me
Are from the face
Of someone else.
Someone else.

So you give me your juice —
The fuel of my flame.
Come take this walk
Through the eyes
Of the whispering face.

Don't give me your blues.
Don't whisper in my face.
Don't tell me no favors.
Don't do me no favors.

There are people I choose,
All for my own —
To see through my eyes,
To become one of the same.

There are people I choose;
They look like you.

To see through my eyes,
To become one of the same.

Don't give me your blues.
Don't whisper in my face.
Don't do me no favors.
Don't do me no favors.

Pinero

I want to tell you a story—
a story of Miguel Piñero,
a poet, a junkie, a man,
a fine man, a true man,
a Puerto Rican.

I watched his story happen
before my eyes.
I laughed,
I cried.
I watched as it went
from happy to sad,
high to low,
low to high,
higher and higher.

But through it all,
he was bad—mallow—
not bad as in *bad,*
but bad as in *good,*
so good it's terrible
that it was bad.
Can you dig?

I seen his good times,
bad times,
high times,

and through it all,
it made me feel alive.

He talked about his trials and ways—
man, you can feel his pain
through that junkie slang.
It helps him to write,
it helps him to create,
it helps him to survive.

It may be the voice
he hears inside,
but no matter what they say,
or what they try to do,
make sure they pour his ashes
on the Lower East Side.

Sister

You're the greatest person I know,
and all I can hope
is that I'll be there, one,
thanking you.

You don't worry about it—
just keep on reading.
And you don't have to understand
why I love you.

There's just no one else
who's like you.
I used to hold your hand—
you always made good of the bad.
I just wanted you to know the truth.

I tried to be just like you.
You know you're the only,
yeah, *you.*

If there was anyone out there
who dreams to be just like you,
I just want you to know
that it's me.

And you do not have to try to
understand—
I just wanted you to know the truth.

I used to hold your hand,
you always made good out of the bad.
I just wanted you to know the truth.

And I know
you'll always be there for me,
and you'll never have to say *I love you,*
because everything you do
is perfect.

I just want you to know
the truth.

Wish

I know my name,
don't ask me how.
I lost my fame —
now I'm on my way down.

Where are the things
that have never been done before?

Through folds,
the shake of the tree
brings the leaves,
stories told.

Which ones
do you want to believe?

Don't ever be
the sounds of your own laughter —
you feel your heartbeat.

I know the pieces
for which you touch,
you know it hurts me.

Don't ever let your feelings
bring you down —
again, they hurt me.

Don't be the person
you wish you weren't.

I know my name,
don't ask me how.
I lost my fame—
now I'm on my way down.

Where are the things
that have never been done before?

Pretend

The air that I breathe,
the soul that I keep,
the deepest admiration
from the anger in my sleep.

So give up the place—
you won't have to see me.
Give up the plate—
you don't have to feed me.
Give up the keys—
you don't have to take me.

Just let me go.

Watch me move without a trace;
you'll never see my face,
no matter what you try to do.
In the end,
they'll bury me in full.

So give up the place—
you won't have to see me.
Give up the plate—
you won't have to feed me.
Give up the keys—
you don't have to take me.

Just let me go.

I see you walking back
with the saddened look upon your
face,
wanting to regain
what has been lost between us.

I see you,
and I'm not being on the same sides.
Now you see what's left inside—
and keep your rhymes and riddles
kept locked away,
and amuse yourself.

Melt

As I melt,
I am right beside you,
for I'm a fool—
a fool who's deep
in your emotions,
whatever the cost.

I'll give my body to you
just for the touch
of your love
and your sweet lips.

If I had you,
there would be no waiting—
no waiting for you.

I grow weak,
your power is strong.
I will use your secrets
to overcome.

But if I had you,
there would be no waiting—
no waiting for you.

As I melt,
I am deep inside you,
for I am a fool—
a fool who's into your emotions.

Now I'm waiting,
waiting for you.

Bones

Come out, come out,
no use in hiding.
Come out, come out,
it's only me—
let me see.

Who were you expecting?
All those bones,
there's no room for me.

Let me help you find
what you need.
Let me be the one
to find today.

Come out, come out,
and kiss the rain.
Come out, come out,
so I can feel your face.

Let me touch
the beauty of human.
Please,
keep me in your mind.

Let me help you find
what you need.
Let me be the one
you find today.

And I see your mistress,
all wrapped up in her headdress,
and the leaves are burning
like the heart I am holding.

Please take these things
and hide them—
no one can find them.

All these bones,
all these bones,
there's no room for me.

No room for me.

Different Views

You—
you've been talking,
saying you're the brains
behind the project.

You—
you've been talking,
loud,
but you still haven't been heard yet.

No.

We all have different views.
Why can't you believe it?
We all have different views.
Oh, why can't you see this?

You—
you walk and talk,
then you fall face first,
right down to the floor.

You—
you said this would make
a man out of me.

Man, keep on trying.
Nobody's listening.

We all have different views.
Oh, why can't you believe it?

17

We all have different views.
Why can't you see this?

Bummed

In this state,
I'm bummed.

No answers.
Tell me what they are teaching—
sacrifice the preachers,
because the smell is on their hands,
hands,
hands.

As I stray from myself,
trapped in my own reason,
trying to be so damn perfect—
but I ran
oh so late,
late,
late.

As I tell this story to myself,
because no one else is listening.

Grasp the wheel of attention,
so I won't be so sacrificed—
scared,
scared,
scared.

As I had a vision
that came right inside my head.

Something—something—
told me to do this one myself,
so I lived through my eyes,
staring directly,
straight ahead.

Nothing will stop me.
I'll do this one myself.

Got any change—
some change,
some change,
some change?

Answers

If I could tell her these answers—
all the ones that were the truth,
the truth that makes me
what I come to be—

I thought they were the answers
only she would know,
only she would know.

Then she came up to me,
asking if I really is me.
I thought only she would know,
she would know.

I said,
don't know what to become of me,
only that this is the brand new me.

Sorry it's not what you used to see.
Please don't tell me
that you're too busy to expect me.

Our love is a building
that can't be broken down.
I just need someone
to say something—
everything's okay.

I can see this ocean
is too wide for one's eyes to see.

I don't make this bed,
that's why I refuse
to lie in it
alone,
alone.

Boil

You said that you would never, ever
lie to me,
And it wasn't contested,
Because I always knew that I could
trust ya.

Well, then you said that you wouldn't
ever cry for me,
And it made me be so angry.
And now you say that you're sorry —
That the truth really hurts ya.

You know these words boil me over,
Pushed to the limit, and fell apart.
I can never trust you again —
But if you come back around, I will.

Well, you took my eyes to a world
where I wander,
To a place where I'm a pushover.
So many ways you can to get back to
start —
But these times are all over,
And I'm crazy, crazy.

You know these words boil me over,
Pushed to a limit, and fell apart.
I can never trust you again —
But if you come back around, I will.

Hole

Anyone who wants to open the hole,
Just put your head down and go.
Gotta want the taste of circumstance—
Then just wash it all away,
Wash it away.

Anything you say,
You know you're getting.
And above all that,
You want even feeling.
Gotta want the taste of every day—
Then wash it away.

I didn't feel the same.
I didn't free the saints.
Gave me a sting—
Felt so fine.
I couldn't see a thing.

As you fall into the zone,
A hazy flower begins to grow.
And all you want is to breathe again.
Whispers open the hole—
Then wash it away.

I didn't feel the same.
I didn't free the saints.
Gave me a sting.

Felt so fine.
I couldn't see a thing.

It's like I don't try to talk,
But things come out the same.
I feel so small,
Like I'm falling out of place.
I can't move at all—
Stuck in an empty space,
Trying to wash it all away.

I didn't feel the same.
I didn't free the saints.
Gave me a sting.
Felt so fine.
I couldn't see a thing.

Sweet Ride

Sudden shake—
Met one time, then turned away.
Lost in tears,
Held my heart against the wind.

Sudden shake—
Found my maker upon the wall.
She turned to me,
Said, *Remember, please,*
How to find your way back to the sun.

'Cause it will make you so sweet and
bright.
Feel for me—feel for me tonight.
'Cause my feeling's goin',
The healin's slowin' down.

Woman speak,
Hanging on every word she says.
Woke from sleep—
One more dream has come to end.

There's something within,
Something within.
Another trip for me,
Then I'll have to say goodbye.

Feel for me—feel for me tonight.
'Cause my feeling's goin',
The healin's slowin' down.

It's been a sweet ride.

Calm

We crossed a life.
It doesn't matter to you.
It matters to me.

We couldn't drift apart,
but we're still floating,
my love.

Now you walk
with your sister in the rain.
I couldn't see
all the good things
through the pain.

I wanted you to be
what I thought I would need.

Where did I go wrong—
in love,
is it fair,
or desire?

You took my hands
through the fire.
I watched you open up
to see the truth
between you and I.

I break down
to save the crown
and smile by mistake.

You tripped out
and didn't look down,
and then pushed me away.

I messed up—
the demons came out.
They just won't go away.

They will never let us fly.
They will never let our love fly—
at least until it's all
gone away,
gone away.

Miss Lovely

To believe it
is to see it—
that's what you told me.

Love, love can be so nice.
To believe it
is to see it.
Love, love can be such a surprise.

There's a reason we're in it.
Love has led us
and will be alright.
There's a reason
to believe it—
and in the end
there is a light.

If you see it,
take it.
Make sure that it's right.

If you're bleeding,
you need it.
We've worked too hard.

I say that's the highest price
for loving
that I've ever seen.

Somebody's bullshit—
you can see right through.
The start of loving
comes from the seed.

I'll be Adam,
you be Eve.

That's the highest price of loving
that I've ever seen—
but you make me buy it
again and again.

The start of loving
comes straight through the seed.
I'll be Adam,
you be Eve—
Miss Lovely.

Hide the Wrong

When the sleeves are long,
you know it hides the wrong.

There's no sound
and no song.

Don't ride the storm,
ride the wrong.

Fearless lives have grown—
hope in this place
so quiet.

Don't leave this one,
stand by the sun.

The even sides
look better
when they're faced
the other way.

When there's no one
who leaves you,
know where I stand—
waiting to be found
and taken
to the passageway.

All I want
is something beautiful,
like diamond eyes

or a pretty face,
porcelain skin,
or an angel
from yesterday.

Cannot see
where I've been,
sands through the hand
of the beauties
that I've had.

I can't forget your name.
Don't ride the storm—
hide the wrong.

September

I know the end
is getting closer,
and in the end
there is no high.

It's life
I'll always remember.
I never wanted this to die.

To see you
tattooed in the sky,
and watch it crystallize
while the salvation
crumbles to dust.

To see the tear
from the unborn child.

Now that it's over,
where do we go?
It's hard beginning
this world alone.

If there was someone—
someone to tell me something,
something to help me
through this disenchanted world—

I want to see,
I want to be free.

Reward

Lovely lady, take my hand and walk
with me.
Lovely lady, let me bring you to peace.
I want you so badly—
So tired of thinking of what could
have been,
And how our world spins around.

Never give up, child.
The best is yet to come.
Never give up—
Your feet won't touch the ground.

And I'm tired of thinking,
Love such a dark cloud.
Never give up, child—
Your soul is safe and sound.
Never give up—
The best is yet to come.

Lovely lady, please come to me.
Lord, I want you so badly.
Lovely lady, take my hand and walk
with me.
I know someday I'll have you.

And I'm tired of waiting—
The more I think of you,

The more I want you around.
These feelings turn me inside out.

Never give up, child—
Your soul is safe and sound.
Never give up, child—
I say the best is yet to come.

I'd build you a heaven
And fill it with all the angels
That are alive on earth—
And take you there
Again and again and again.

Lovely lady,
Walk with me.

Look Back

Look back, where we roam with the
trees,
But never, never bloom.
Where all the leaves from the weather
start its birth—
Burnt to toast, everlasting glow.

Laugh longer than a lifetime,
Shake and leave for now and forever.
It's better than a palm read,
Just to know it's real—
Burnt to toast, everlasting glow.

Wanted all that is expected to be,
Life through the birds and the bees.
I showed stare, but you don't care.
Can't you see my punches are bee
stings?
They won't hurt you—no, they won't
hurt.

You don't need space,
If the laughs are still there.
I'll be waiting, I'll be waiting.

Please look back again,
Where we roam with the trees,
But never, never bloom.
I'll be waiting, I'll be waiting.

Love a Steal

You never knew what would come of
that velvet grade.
You never felt the light until the sun
slapped your face.
You didn't know what you wanted,
But you plead your case.
You wiped your face —
You couldn't do it.

No innocent past.
Show your colors and leave what you
had.
Please, please —
Be who you want to be.
Know your history.
'Cause my love's for real.
Does that make my love a steal?

'Cause love — love is all that I have left.
Like a pretender with no morals,
I'm swept away.

I ask for words,
But you only moan
Now that the sound circulates.
How much longer do I have to wait?

'Cause my love's for real—
Doesn't that make my love a steal?
'Cause love, love is all that I have left.

It's soooo sad—
Like a poet on his last page,
Or life on its last day.
It makes the angels cry
When the music dies.
It's their pride and joy—
Their baby boy.

Loud Silence

Well, I'm on my way to a future up
above,
And I'm going to lay on the pillow in
the sky—
Because I feel no pain,
No more tears in my eyes.

See, I lost my mind,
Fell apart at the seams,
Looked and seen that no one was
around—
Except maybe me,
And this, my disease.

LOUD, I'm no longer silent.
LOUD, I stopped from falling.
LOUD, I'm no longer silent.
LOUD, I stopped from falling down.

People said they were used to seeing
me
With my face to the ground,
And that they would bury me
Before my time came around.

Well, I've seized the day,
Made the changes that were right.
I found faith in me—

And now the future is so bright,
And I shout.

Bed of Roses

My mind's dreaming in the middle of
the day.
She reads the winds—
The doves are her fate.
Moments are what matter.

She's been on my mind
As I sit by her,
Staring eye to eye,
Smiling at a good girl.
She's all I want.
Everything's coming up roses.

Looking at her green eyes,
It felt just like the sunlight.
A bed of roses
Is where I want to lie.

She walks by so lovely—
The paint of her dress
Is a vision I'll never forget.
Looking at the good girl,
She's what I want.
Everything's coming up roses.

Floated Shower Wreck

Tears of the mother belong to the sky,
Tearing to pieces alone with the wind.
Heroes in stretchers—where is my
home?
So close the doors and climb the walls.

Tear your shadow down.
Remember to forget
All the things you hate, your shame.
But there's so much pain.

When I hear you say
That you want to disappear
someday—
Someday.

Don't mind the day.
Don't pass away.
Tearing to pieces alone with the wind.
I'll never walk away.
I won't pretend.

Seen It All

Met a man
dressed in a cloth
where the roads have crossed.

Stuck out his hand,
extended honor,
and gave this final thought:

Stay on the right path.
Don't get sidetracked.
It's for a very good cause —
to find the truth
and fly again,
to love without a fault.

He said,
I've seen it all, he told me.
Seen the light.
Seen it all, he told me.
Seen the light.

So I took his word,
strayed from the curve,
and jumped from cloud to cloud.

Sat on the sun,
never got burned,
never took a fall.

That grateful speech
kept me on my feet.

Now I sing this song—
seen it all.
Seen it all.

If I never say goodbye,
would you love me forever?

If I lied,
would you remember
how we would always be together?

Because now I can't remember
all the love.
Because I surrendered
to all the things
that made me render—
to all the looks in the mirror
that told me
I wouldn't last forever.

But till the end of the world
and the end of time,
or the last thing I see—
my heart is yours.

Please hold it
and don't cry.
I may be never coming home,
never coming home.

Please hold it
and don't cry,
because you'll always be mine.

Just remember
that you're not alone,
because the memories
of you and me
are so tender.

But I made you cry.
I didn't mean
to leave you all alone.

But I scream
at the top of my lungs,
and from the top of the world —

but I made you cry.

You cried.

I Hope to Be Okay

As I'm writing in the afternoon,
making the change,
I won't pick up
the pieces of the past—
they've disappointed
into flames.

For the wishes
that are inside of me,
I hope to be okay.

So I put it all to rest quickly,
because I just want
this day to stay.

Looking at the sky,
dreaming,
wondering why
it's so neutral,
and where does it get
its strength?

Strength,
where were you
when I spilled over?

We couldn't all
crawl out of the door.

Please take this boy
out of this town.

Some of us
are fancy
in our own ways.
We all seem
a little cynical.

But there's no one to blame.

Me—
I will take all the stars
and be the sky
I want to be,
shining
for you and me.

As I wait for you
on this afternoon,
it takes me to no means.

Is this the space
that makes you comfortable?

I look for you in a dream.
If you're not there,
I will wrap myself in flames
to keep you warm
until you return again.

I know there is more for us.

Lovely—
I'm just beginning
to be a man.

I made a list.

Dig

Give me something I can touch.
To be nothing is such a bore.
Why can't I believe in me?
And inside I'm so hollow.

So give me faith
To see me doing something else —
But these things that hurt me.
I turn to the sky and ask for help,
And then...

God told me!
This is real life — feel alive.
God told me!
Stop the fighting and see the light — be
delight.

To take something that isn't mine,
To eat it up and spit it out,
To live something so vain,
To take it and throw it all away —
And inside I'm so hollow.

So give me back to me,
Because inside I'm so hollow.

God told me!
This is real life — feel alive.
God told me!

Stop the fighting and see the light—be
delight.

Harder

Yours is the kiss that makes me grow
weak.
My head hangs down and my body
aches.
Pushing makes my love grow
stronger—
Makes my heart beat harder.

Nothing else will keep me awake.
My head hangs low—there's no
mistake.
Pushing makes my love grow
stronger.

There's no real reason.
There's no real taste.
There's no real feelings.
You're such a disgrace.

Yours is the kiss that keeps me awake.
I'm up all night because my body
aches.
Yours is the touch that makes me
complete.
My head hangs low and my body
aches.

Sweet thing.
No worries.

We'll stay up all night.
No worries.
No need to be uptight.

Pushing makes the heart grow
fonder —
Keep pushing harder.

Gunfight

My life is a gunfight—
Not self-centered,
But caught in a scene
Of to do wrong or to do right.

Will they ever catch me?
Or just pass by without a flaunt?
Either way,
I'll hold my head up high.

If you really want to know me,
Take a chance and roll the dice.
Lucky number seven or a crap out—
That's the test of faith in me.

NOW! comes the end,
Where we say our goodbyes
And see how good God has made
us—
And say a prayer.

NOW! don't pretend
That you can think for you
Or the rest of us—
Saying a prayer.

NOW! comes the end,
Where we say goodbye
And see how good God has made

us—
Say a prayer.

NOW! NOW!

After All

That one moment when she cries—
I cry all night.
That may sound strange to some.
She swears it will be done
When one tear hits the ground,
And she aims to go back to herself—
To herself.

When she's tired from desire,
Of this life she's been waiting too long,
And the time spins around,
And all that she wants
Is to hear the chimes of her favorite
song—

Oh, but after all, after all,
If I fall, I fall for her.

I try and I try,
But if I leave, she will never be found.
Well, I'm tired, and I'm tired
Of keeping this alive.
It's a shame that it's bringing you
down.
Yeah.

Oh, but after all, after all,
If I fall, I fall for her.

Oh, this love is going to break my
soul.
Morning falls,
And it means nothing to no one—
That the tears in my eyes will never
fall.
I must be strong.

My turn

This Is My Story

Don't tell me it's not true.
You weren't there.

Now that you've heard,
what would you do?

I write about my life.
I write about what I feel,
what I've lived,
what I've seen,
what makes me laugh,
what makes me cry.

I'm sorry it was about you.
Deal with it.

I write obliviously
about my mother,
my father,
and my sisters,
and what it's all about.

Not bad,
but good—
because it's all experience.

I would never give
any of this up.
I like the me I've become.

Why can't you?

Because you've made me.

Why ask why?
That's just the way
it is sometimes.

Our words disappear.
Maybe that's the way
it should have been.

Forget all the things
we should have been.

We spoke in riddles
and never found out why—
but we were always
looking for a home.

That's the one thing
that mattered to me.

Home

You'll never know
if the stars will shine.
You don't know
when the sun will go down.

Taking those steps
where tomorrow
will bring you back
to the home
where you belong.

I drove all night
to get back to you.
I always said
I will be back someday.

But when I found
my way back home,
you were gone—
you were gone.

The city watched me walk away,
but kept a light on for me.
Kept it lit
and held it high,
never to let it go out.

Kept my memory alive
and never let it go.

Leave me,
but don't forget me.

You'll never know
if the sun will shine
or the stars will shine.

Ah—
taking those steps
where tomorrow
will bring you back
to the home
where you belong.

Take my hand,
we'll fly away,
to keep our dream
from running away.

Leave me,
but don't forget me.

Images

Why can't I keep this
From becoming a great big fucking
hoax?
How can I keep my kids
From coming from a broken home?

There are all these keys,
But none of them open the door.
Cried to the innocent —
They didn't want images.

Never to learn,
Never to live,
Never to love.

Couldn't sleep at times.
In my bed, I'm all alone.
It makes me wish
For the things I can only hope.

Why can't I keep this all to myself?
Tried to be innocent —
All I got was images.

Never the same.
No one to blame,
No one to blame.

420

420,
a smoker's holiday —
almost like booze
on St. Patrick's Day,
but this is a holiday
called Fried day.

Light up a blunt
like every other day.
Time to get high.
Don't let this day go by.

From the hour I woke up
to the hour I passed out —
don't tell me I'm wrong.
It keeps me strong.
It helps me rhyme
the words to my songs.

420,
a smoker's holiday.
Blazing, hazing,
like any other day.

420,
the weed holiday.
Smoke it up
every other day.

As She Is in Mine

Nothing left to do
But to blow a kiss to you
And wave our last goodbye.

I woke up teary-eyed,
Because all that's left behind
Are these photographs of you.

Can't get back to the norm —
It's the weather before the storm.
Thought I'd really got to try.

Love, don't let me down —
Our day will come.
My smile has turned upside down.
There's no morning sun,
So love, don't let me down.
Our day will come.

There's nothing like your heart.
I wish it didn't stop
Feeling love for me.

Our dreams have come and gone.
There's nothing that can be done,
So I'll just walk away.

Love, don't let me down —
Our day will come.
My smile has turned upside down.

There's no more sun,
So love, don't let me down.
Our day will come.

Forget, Forgotten

I see my dreams.
I play my song—
The only way I know how to release it.
Every day I keep this inside,
But when I tell you,
You just can't seem to believe it.

Nothing to say—
Your mouth to the floor.
These are the times that I'm receiving.
Caught in a daze,
No way to keep busy.
That means nothing to me—
I've got to keep moving.

I look back and see you crawling,
Trying to catch up to me running.
Miss me when I'm gone,
Because baby, after all,
If it's not what I'm believing,
Catch me if I fall.

There's so much to miss.
You don't really care.
But one thing—
Never forget my name.
Please, never forget my name.

Reprise

How will we end the day?
Your favorite scent,
your favorite way?

Will we live and fly,
where the flowers lie?
Will we never know?
Well, we must try.

The trouble is
that life's too fast.
Let's save our lovin'
and make it last.

When we close our eyes,
we take a trip
to the other side.

Isn't this what we dream about?
We've got to keep on saying
that one day we'll be alive.

I've been in love for the pain,
and it brought my name
in front of God.

And she said,
the guilt is not to be forsaken.

And I realized—
to make a little love,
not space.

Isn't this what we dream about?
We've got to keep on saying
that one day we'll be alive,
that one day
it will come to life.

Scratches

Take a trip
through a worried mind.
See the glimpse
of troubled times.

From the sea
to the ocean side,
I've tried
to fool mankind.

They wouldn't let me
get away with this.
All the pain you see
is mine.

Took a dream by my side later—
she took my hand
because she believed in me,
and I walked her
through the pain.

But it was not her game.
She was better than me.

Scratches on the surface.
I feel like I deserve this.

You're so confused
because I lied.

Serve no purpose
but to make you cry.

So you cried on my fields,
planted the tree
that will always grow.

My mind is a wheel,
spinning in circles.
I've lost everything.

Please—
raise your hands,
pick up your things,
and run from me.

Scratches on the surface.
I feel like I deserve this.

You're so confused
because I lied.
Serve no purpose
but to make you cry.

Tell Me

Touch the bruised —
You are carved in stone.
They come from each of you.
I'm stuck with pins.
The latest is a lie.
Can't begin to be humble.
These wounds won't heal in time.
Empty spots, yet I still crumble.

Tell me —
Can you heal the fallen sun?
Cut from hope, never to be done.
Can you keep these walls from caving
in?
Take the itch away —
Don't want to start again.

Can you heal the fallen sun?
Cut from hope, never to be done.
Let's get off this road of disbelief.
Fall asleep — never to wake again.

Tell me.
Nearer and nearer that I walk,
Blood spills from me
Because I'm torn from all the jabbing
pins.
This hole is between us.

I'll never toy with the hands of
another.

Many times I've turned to rust—
Blood for grace,
Sweat to dust,
The essence for the stone.
Even though it's just you,
You know you're not alone.

Hellish jackpot, pilled within—
Cure this itch the way I can,
To fall in love with life again,
To fall in love with life again.

Leaves Me Not

Here, but it's not me.
Blind, but I can see.
Took hits from the woman
And lost someone who believed.

Whole, but not complete.
Bound, but set free.
Felt like the water
That had been flushed away.

Near, but you can't see.
Smile in tragedy.
Kept from the moment
And sent so far away.

My head hits the ground
When you're around.
It's hip, but feels so lame.
My lips are bit,
My hair is all pulled out.
It used to go away —
Now it leaves me not.

Leaves me not.
It leaves me not a thing.

Legend, but unknown.
Faith, but no belief.

Then came the moment
That left an empty space.

Knocked out, but I'm awake.
Burning as I freeze.
Fell from the world
And then felt born again.

Stellar

So I'm screaming out to you,
Straight back from the bitter wake—
Stuck hanging on a memory.
Why? I just don't know.
(You know. You know.)

I still want your love,
But it's so damn far away.
And not without affection,
And where we're not alone.
And it's good,
Because I wasn't built that way.

I seem to have just gotten over life,
And it feels good not to feel that
way—
The way that left you stellar,
Hoping for something better.

I seem to be over life lies.
The clouds have been parted.
(Run, run, run away with me.)

They've been split into two roads—
The high and the low.
And we've been down both of those.
But let us both be free,
No matter where short cuts may take
us.

Let's take our time and pay our dues,
And it's good.

Wings

Feeling so alone,
Trying to find a home
With both of my eyes closed.
I took the road of low —
I'm not just blowing smoke.

My life's never been the same.
I feel the demons getting close.
I know they won't be prone
To the faith I have inside.

The lights have been turned off,
The candles are burnt out,
And I'm left with nowhere to go.

But now the leaves will fall.
Come afternoon, night, or dawn —
I've got to stay awake.
I've lost track of time,
But I've never paid it no mind.
The years have been blown away.

Now you've upped and gone —
I know I'll still live on
With this one wish upon my wings.

Walk this road alone
With feelings that have grown.
In everything I need,

The truth will all unfold
To find purity of the soul,
So I can earn my wings.

Honey

You're smooth like honey.
I saw the drips last night
Because the fires were burning.

You came dear to me
And quickly stunned me,
But you shouldn't try to own me —
And that scares you as you run away.
But you know my heart will find you.

You'll remember me, my honey.
I'll put my heart inside you.
My big secret was to win you over,
Because you're so smooth, my honey.

When lit, you see me,
Covered by the stars.
The dreams I am receiving
Have spaces for two hearts —
The source of sweet relief and reality.

As I step myself across the bridge,
I'm fooled once again.

Oh, my honey, you're so smooth.
You'll remember me, my honey.
I'll put my heart inside you.
My big secret was to win you over,
Because you're so smooth, my honey

Give

I was in mind today,
Looking out the mirrored way—
The cuts on my surface almost
defined,
As I vowed to give thanks
By the other's surprise.

I bow to my knees,
Loosen the crown.
The bliss on my face
Pushes the ground.

Now the haunt of your arms
Are so far away.
Mind of the pure
Is something they could not give.

Energy gains,
United by fear—
If only I endured the years.

Every time I caught up
To your mystery,
You only repeated whispers.
(I could not hear you.)

Drown as We Breathe

A broken vein that cannot breathe,
A voice that screamed but could not
be seen.
I struggled to find the ground —
I plowed into the ground.

So many lines have been crossed,
But I still was not found.
My voice would shout,
My voice was so loud,
Yet I could not be found.

I struggled to fly out,
But as I screamed inside,
We are sweat-eyed.
As I hold so tight,
I will not deny.
I will face the light.
I will not die.

I think only of you and I.
I hear our song in every melody.
It's about love.
It's about being free.
I drown as we breathe.
Drown as we breathe.

I'll sing till the high notes die.
My voice is a roar tonight.

Nothing can hold us down—
We fight back loud.

Wishful Times

As I keep shaking,
There's no hope at all.
God only helps me—
I don't even have to ask.

All I've took for granted
Has run out on me,
Filled the cup over the edge.

As I look back in my mind,
Oh, it kept me alive.
In this world, I live alone.
Oh, let me lie.

Oh, I hoped till the well was gone dry,
And the tears have dried.
Oh, the sun was the time
When you held to me and cried.

Oh, wishful times,
When you take my head for flight.
I wish to myself
As I begin to crack this empty shell—
Don't even ask.
Oh, I'll be fine.

Wallowed

The day came crashing
like God's fist to the earth.

No real changes—
just the same old dirt.

What hope,
all the things we could do—
the way we share,
the way we love,
to hold the challenges we absorb.

If you're anything but sure,
turn and run from me.
I know it hurts,
but it's worth the wait.

Stop hiding,
stop hiding.

The way we share,
the way we love,
to hold the challenges we absorb.

If we could live
vigorously and pure,
our worlds would stop colliding.

Just like you,
I want to die on this earth.

Please stop hiding—
hiding.

Lifeless Moment

Gonna set all the basics
To start it up again.
It's all so deceiving,
It's all a disguise.

Maybe if we shot down to the places—
Maybe mine are different to me.
Oh, I'll stay awake every night,
Awake till we're both out to sea.
Yeah, you and me.

The wildest come home,
You make the weepiest frown.
It's a lifeless moment,
Recovering from the saddest night.
All the realists want to know
If I'm gonna come down.

Among those who recognize it,
All the desperate places—
She acts just like a baby,
Just to wash it all away.

But in these places,
We all hope to see ourselves
As human beings.
We're such crazy, selfish monkeys.

God, if it were just you and me—
Message to you, see, see shooting
stars.
They're here to take us for a ride.

It's such a lifeless moment,
Recovering from the saddest nights.
It'll take a lifetime for certain,
Recovering from the saddest nights.

But all the realists want to know
Is if we're gonna come down,
Down,
Down,
Down.

Man

All alone I seem to break.
I stare, and the mirror starts to crack.
My eyes won't shut.
I can't blink.
Does that make me not a man?

I'm not the only one who believes.
Push myself to succeed.
Take that life—
That's not for me.
I've done all this the best I can.
Does that make me not a man?

I'm not only the person that I believe,
I'm the only person you perceive.
Burned a fire from gasoline,
Drove a thousand miles with no sleep.

Trying to make it through the daily
mend,
Trying hard to be a man.

All alone I plead my case.
Where the air's out, I feel safe.
I hope that I've done you no harm.
I'm sorry it took so long.

I just feel like it was time to make a
stand—

Time to make it right.
Now I'm waiting to be a man.

To be continued.

Over and Over

The grease has turned into steam.
There's too much smoke—can't
breathe.
It's just the same thing
Over and over and over.

So when you're sick and tired,
Hands burned from the fire,
And you keep feeling the same thing
Over and over and over—

When these thoughts turn into
disease,
Give life to your dreams,
And keep telling yourself
The same thing
Over and over and over.

So get up on your feet,
And stand up and scream—
They can't do this to me!
And keep telling yourself
The same thing
Over and over and over.

My eyes are open,
So I can see,
And I won't do

The same thing
Over and over and over.

My Child

My mind may not be complete
Without breath and sleep.
I'll wait here for you.

Our lives —
We don't know who's more taboo.
Your face and skin,
You've been keeping for the one
Who can break your heart.

Cannot believe
You're the piece of my heart that's
missing.
Cannot believe
You're taking this all so peacefully.
Cannot see your faults through my
eyes.
Don't shake me at any time —
This must be a dream.

Armed with the crimes that make us
done,
You're so complete —
There's so much for us.
Now we try to stay alive
Through the hope, fear, and pride.
And we'll try until the chains won't
win,

And we're born again,
My child.

I ask — who do you love and pry?
Who do you need?
Words, don't try to move.
I've heard this all before —
What's real, and what tears us apart.

My child,
Cannot believe
You're the piece of my heart that's
missing.
Cannot believe
You're taking this all so peacefully.
Cannot see your faults through my
eyes.
Don't shake me at this time —
This must be a dream.

M, F, L

Alone,
I cut my face.
Cut the skin,
take the pain.

Alone,
I break my hand,
smash the mirror,
take the stand.

This is not the way
I've seen my life —
living all of this
out of spite.

Alone,
I take my faith,
keeping this inside
with no escape.

I know everything
but can't explain.
Try to put this
all into frame.

It's such a sad picture
that I paint —
all alone in my place,

kept from love,
met with hate.

My mind tends to pay
for these feelings
that I fake.

I cannot begin to explain
just who I am.

Sometimes you go away,
sometimes you come
with the pain.

What a critical price to pay.
I guess I wasn't part of the deal.

All the mistakes
may come and go,
but this hell
I cannot stand.

Breeze

There are things that make us whole—
Only you can take control
Of the truth, the truth.

Nothing will take the absence
Of the only man
That can make you understand.

I ask, how pretty are you?
And the blush feels like the love or
breeze.
And what will be of the girl?
She has me,
As she is taken from the seed.

Soul and girl—
No one is the breeze.

On the street of love,
She wears the place like the one being.
On love street,
The girl is one being *(God)*.

There is nothing but the being of the
woman
That will make me
The man I want to be.

My Child

My mind may not be complete
Without breath and sleep.
I'll wait here for you.

Our lives—
We don't know who's more taboo.
Your face and skin,
You've been keeping for the one
Who can break your heart.

Cannot believe
You're the piece of my heart that's
missing.
Cannot believe
You're taking this all so peacefully.
Cannot see your faults through my
eyes.
Don't shake me at any time—
This must be a dream.

Armed with the crimes that make us
done,
You're so complete—
There's so much for us.
Now we try to stay alive
Through the hope, fear, and pride.
And we'll try until the chains won't
win,

And we're born again,
My child.

I ask—who do you love and pry?
Who do you need?
Words, don't try to move.
I've heard this all before—
What's real, and what tears us apart.

My child,
Cannot believe
You're the piece of my heart that's
missing.
Cannot believe
You're taking this all so peacefully.
Cannot see your faults through my
eyes.
Don't shake me at this time—
This must be a dream.

Reflecting

I will sit and think a thought or two,
Then have a drink and start off new.
I'll think of the day,
I'll think of the night—
I will see the sun that shines so bright.

By the ocean I will stay,
Looking at the sky.
I will lay there
Till the day passes by.

If you can come and lay with me,
You will see
You can have good thoughts
Just like me.

Miracle

Looks like the miracle
Has lost its way home.
I wait for the call
On the telephone.

Now that the fear
Has been exposed,
Now that the year
Has left me alone.

My head hits the ground,
Now my hair is all pulled out.
The things going around —
The morning was on its way.

Looks like the miracle
Has lost its way home.
My woman calls me
On the radio
Because I love
The beauty of music.

Everything's fine now —
The baby sleeps.
I couldn't handle this alone.

My head hits the ground,
Now my hair is all pulled out.

The things going around—
The morning was on its way.

Love was the look
On my face,
My face.

A Place for Me

Well, I'm going to buy a car
And tackle the road.
I might even take a bus
Just to watch the wheels roll.

Maybe I'll take a plane
Just to rise above.
I might even take a boat
Just to watch it float,
Or a train
To see the coast.

I'll climb a mountain
Just to look down,
Because I live close to the ground.

So I'm going to find a place
That has no bounds.
Maybe there's a place
Where no one frowns—
A place where there are no gray
clouds.

A place for me.
A place we can all see
Without care.
See things
That will leave us without despair.

Say the things
I've been waiting to hear
Throughout the year—
The things that prove you care.

Any place
That will have me as is.
And say the things.

That's it.
I've got to turn it back on.
I've got to start over again.

See—and I don't know where it cut
off,
So I can't start it.

A Place We Can All See

A place we can all see
Without a care—
See the things
That will have us
Without despair,
The things
That prove you care.

Girl

Girl, girl,
Do you remember
When I was your world?
I was your light—
I was your brightest star.

Now the times
Have turned so cruel.
A whole new world,
A place that
Makes us apart.
How did our love
Lose your heart?

But I remember the days
When we were whole.
Kisses were sold—
We talked about eternity.

Now the times have changed,
Turned so cruel.
The things we forget to do.

It doesn't seem fair,
This life of ours.
And when you are alone,
And whenever you look back,
We might have been stars.

Shadow

I walk among the living,
But no one knows I'm here.
No one wants to know,
And no one really cares.

I am but a shadow
Who really walks the streets.
I walk along the very poor
And sometimes the very elite.

I could pass out on the sidewalk,
Or I could even die.
I am but a shadow —
And no one really cares.

I'm not just here.
I am everywhere.

I am homeless.

Ashes

I'll take my memories at the seams
And keep them in my dreams.
Take care of what I had
And make me glad I'm where I am.

Forgive me for what I've done—
I thought I was the powerless one.
That was then,
This is now.
I'll take a stand
And take a bow.

Don't tell me anything left out.
See things
For what they're all about.

Confused Man

Why do I feel
Like a stranger
In my own town?
Somebody tell me
What's going down.

I can't sleep,
I can't eat,
I can't think.
My days were lost
In just a wink.

Just turn away
And let me be.
Go ahead
And tell me lies
Until you realize
You were not very wise.

Let time wash away
My tears
And love lost,
So I can face my fears
And overcome them
At any cost

Lovely Lady (Revised Poem Version)

Lovely lady,
Let me bring you to peace.
I want you so badly—
Tired of thinking
Of what could have been
And the world we evolve around.

Never give up, child.
The best is yet to come.
Never give up—
Your feet won't touch the ground.

Tired of thinking
That love is such a dark cloud.
Never give up, child—
Your soul is safe and sound.
Never give up.
The best is yet to come.

Lovely lady in my dreams,
Please come to me.
I want you so badly.

Lovely lady,
Take my hand
And walk with me.
Someday I'll have you.

The more I think of you,
The more I want you around.
This feeling
Turns my love inside out.

Never give up now —
Your soul is safe and sound.
Never give up, child.
The best is yet to come.

Rules

Loneliness is a state of mind
And not a way to be.

Fright is just a feeling
And not something you see.

Spirit is a form of pride
In the things you do and say.

Vanity is what people should hide,
For it takes your heart away.

Beauty is a valuable thing—
Not to be bought or sold.
And once you get it in your life,
It's worth more than gold.

That Day

Someday we will be together—
True love never dies.
On you
I could always rely.

We are but two separate souls,
And I know
We will become whole.

I wait for that day
So I can be by your side.

You ask me not to wait,
But I will trust my heart—
Not even time
Can keep us apart.

My Girl Gorgeous

I lost my girl gorgeous—
She went away from me.
I thought I was perfect,
Thought I had everything.

Never did I get excited,
Never did I ignore.
Make these things not happen,
Or I can't take this anymore.

I lost my girl gorgeous—
The greatest thing on my mind.
Things won't get any better
Until she's by my side.

Never did I get excited,
Never did I ignore.
Make these things not happen,
Or I can't take this anymore.

In the end I'm crying,
Begging to have more.
I can't take the silence
As she walked out the door.

Never did I see this,
Or never did I want anymore.
Why did this have to happen?
I can't take this anymore.

Never did I see this,
Or I just thought to ignore.
Now that it's not happening,
I'm left on the floor.

Never did I get excited,
Never did I ignore.
Make these things not happen,
Or I can't take it anymore

Stay With Me

Once there was a time
When you and me were kind.
But now those days are old—
They've all turned to stone.

But please stay with me.
Please stay with me.

Fearing the losses
That you hide,
Knowing once
And feeling twice.

You can run,
But you can't hide.

I dream all day,
I walk all night—
Waiting for the day
That I will have you.

And in the morning
I'm alone,
Waiting for the day
They'll bring me home
To you.

Please stay with me.
Stay with me.

Free Yourself

Every single memory—
The feelings you have,
Good or bad—
You can fall in love,
And I'm sure
Everything will turn out all right.

Free yourself
If there's nothing to do.
If you can't sleep tonight,
Look to the sky
And wish upon a star.

You will see everything clear
And find out
Who you really are.

So free yourself.

Wonder

Once in love,
You change your face—
It chases the demons
Out of this place.

Love changes the rain
That brings a mirror to the sky.
Love brings happy tears
That fall like drops
In your eyes.

Wonder if it can be told
That real love
Is like a piece of gold—
It's priceless
And it's true,
Like the love
I have for you.

The Ocean

When things seem to go wrong,
The ocean side
Is where I belong.

Something about the breeze
Of the tide
Is comfort to the soul
And has nothing to hide.

Take me to the place
Where no one can see
The pain in my eyes
And the fear within me.

With every grain
Of ocean sand
There is a new creation
Of a far-away land.

I'll go to my place
So no one will know—
By the ocean sand
And sunrise glow.

Beautiful Lie

It's been a while,
But it feels like you've never left.
The years gone by
Have only brought us closer.

We have this moment blessed —
But it's a beautiful lie.
It's only for this one time
You'll be faced
With this beautiful lie.

Nice girl
With a devil inside —
I don't mind
The beautiful lie.

Play the game,
But you beat me to it.
It's only for this one time.
It might be worth it —
This beautiful lie.

We bring out
The devil inside,
But there was a place to hide.

Even after
Our last kiss goodbye,
I know it all

Had to be
A beautiful lie.

Masterpiece

There is a story —
A story about a woman,
A woman we all know,
A woman full of life,
A woman full of love.

She dazzles you
With her charm.
She turns the world
Upside down.

She shines
Like a masterpiece.
She makes the walls
Crumble to the ground.

With a subtle smile
And a warm glance,
She can pleasure you
For a while.
She'll make
Your heart dance.

I must confess
This story is true —
Because in the end
This woman
Is you.

My masterpiece.

Leave Me Not

I'm here, but it's not me.
Blind, but I can see.
Took hits from the woman
And lost someone who believes.

Whole, but not complete.
Bound, but set free.
Felt like the water
That's been flushed under me.

My head hits the ground
When you're around.
It's hip,
But it feels so lame.
My lips are bit,
My hair pulled out.
I used to go away—
Now it leaves me not.

Legend, but unknown.
Faith, but no belief.
Then came the moment
That led me to believe.

Knocked out, but awake.
Burning as I freeze.
I hit the ground
When you're around.
It's hip,

But it feels so lame.
My lips are bit,
My hair pulled out.
I used to go it all away.

Movin' on

In the morning,
seeing my dove fly away —
should have never gone.

I'll treat you right
after all I've done wrong.
Trust in what I say.

Sugar, don't go.
I've been left alone,
but I'm praying —
praying on my own.
Oh, the pain.

It's too early
to pack your bags,
to leave me alone.
Get to your home.

Baby's ready for a change.
Didn't mean to do you wrong.

Sugar, don't go.
I've been left alone.
Now I'm praying —
praying on my own.
Oh, the pain.

Sure Shot Lady

Lady of the night.
Come on,
the feeling is right.

Your heart says yes,
but your mind says no.
You try to hide it,
but everybody knows.

You're a sure shot lady.
You drive yourself crazy.
Sure shot lady.

You know it's not right,
so deep in the night.
Sure shot lady.

Good girl gone bad.
Sure shot lady.

Back to the crib
for fun and games.
After tonight,
you'll notice he's the same.

Growing up,
you were told to say no,
but after that first time,
it was go, go, go —
for what's done is done.

Now you're a sure shot lady,
driving yourself crazy.
Sure shot lady.

You know it's not right,
so deep in the night.
Sure shot lady.

Take a number
and wait
for the sure shot lady.

Sure shot lady —
people call
because they know it's right.

Lonely men
will pay the price.

You wish you could go back
to the way things were
years ago.

Stick with me,
and I'll take you home.

Feelings

My life was a cloud
before I met her.
She changed my way of thinking.

If you try hard enough,
you can do it.
If you don't,
you go nowhere.

I stand without a tear
in my heart alone.
Maybe not even a sound
will rumble.

Music fills my head
along with dreams.
The two together
make me happier than ever.

If you can fulfill your dreams,
then keep trying
until you do.
Live out your dreams.

Nothing can stop you
from dreaming.
Sometimes that's all you've got.

Dreams are wild
and crazy.

Sometimes scary
and horrible.
Some are so terrific
you don't want to wake up.

Thoughts are nothing to waste.
Share your thoughts.
Don't be afraid
of what you feel.

If love is the answer,
time must be a great question.

Been Thinking

I've been thinking about you and I.
Been thinking about the good times
and the times you cried.

We were having a sweet fit
when you caught my eye.
Reality set in
with honesty by my side.

I ask you:
don't take this out of hand,
and don't say you had no chance.

But lately,
I've been thinking about you.
Lately,
I've been thinking about you and I.

Been thinking about the bad times
and the times when you were sad.
Now hugs, not kisses —
but when you came around,
nothing but space between us,
even our own common ground.

And I ask you
not to take this so out of hand,
and don't say you had no chance.

But lately,
I've been thinking about you and I.

There are days you're mine —
you go down again
and again
and again.

The coin has turned
to the other side.
You had your chance
and refused to reply.

But lately,
I've been thinking about you and I.

Just Give Up

You test me
with your war of words
because you think I'll fall.
You might as well quit
while you're ahead.
My brain's not so small.

Don't insult me.
I'm the one behind the wheel
of my mind of rage.
My shit can go for miles.

You won't be able to speak.
Better grab a seat —
this ride is going to be wild.
So you should step back
before you feel the pain.

I must warn you:
I'll make you piss your pants,
scare you cold,
and when you try to react,
your story's already old.

You'll say,
poor, twisted me.

So now, just give up.
I'll ask you — please —

just give up.
On your knees,
just give up.

Stay in your little world.
Stay back from my path.
You've buried yourself in a hole,
and there's no turning back.

Go home, boy.
I'll ask you — please —
just give up.

He's the One

He's the one.

There in the distance
lies a man so powerful and unique
that no one can compete.

He will show the way —
things you never seem to believe.
He's the one to show.

You know it's done
in ways you've never seen or heard.
He's the one,
the greatest one of all.

He's the one —
so raise your hand and shout.
He'll guide the way
for a better day.

He's the one you'll need,
so don't beg or plead.

I think there is nothing left.
I pull up a chair,
pour me a glass —
don't stop until the end
or until I'm dead
trying to discover what I need.

There's something I want.
There's something out there
that will change me.

Wherever I Want to Go

Mornings are easy,
The night's long.
I've waited my life
To be this strong.

It's been a long time—
My hopes have been gone,
But the love of the music
Has helped me live on.

There comes a moment
In a man's life
Where he has to make up his mind
Or pack up and go home.

But this is my chance
Not to stand alone.

For one night
I want to shout
And tell the world
I'm a man with no way out.

I've taken the high road,
Lived on the low road—
But my heart
Will always take me
Wherever I want to go.